ANCIENT GREECE

Philip Steele

KINGFISHER
LONDON & NEW YORK

Copyright © Kingfisher 2011
Published in the United States by Kingfisher,
175 Fifth Ave., New York, NY 10010
Kingfisher is an imprint of Macmillan Children's Books, London.
All rights reserved.

Distributed in the U.S. by Macmillan,
175 Fifth Ave., New York, NY 10010

Library of Congress Cataloging-in-Publication data has been applied for.

Consultant: Dr. Hugh Bowden, King's College London, U.K.

Illustrations by: Thomas Bayley, Peter Bull Art Studio, Gary Hanna (www.the-art-agency.co.uk),
Roger Stewart, Steve Stone (Artist Partners Ltd.), Steve Weston (Linden Artists)

ISBN: 978-0-7534-6579-0

Kingfisher books are available for special promotions and premiums.
For details contact: Special Markets Department, Macmillan,
175 Fifth Ave., New York, NY 10010.

For more information, please visit www.kingfisherbooks.com

Printed in China
1 3 5 7 9 8 6 4 2
1TR/0311/UG/WKT/140MA

Note to readers: The website addresses listed in this book are correct at the time of publishing.
However, due to the ever-changing nature of the Internet, website addresses and content can change.
Websites can contain links that are unsuitable for children. The publisher cannot be held responsible for
changes in website addresses or content or for information obtained through third-party websites.
We strongly advise that Internet searches should be supervised by an adult.

**The Publisher would like to thank the following for permission to reproduce their material. Every care has been taken to trace copyright holders.
However, if there have been unintentional omissions or failure to trace copyright holders, we apologize and will, if informed, endeavor to make
corrections in any future edition. (t = top, b = bottom, c = center, r = right, l = left):**

Front cover tl Alamy/The Art Gallery Collection; tr Getty/Digital Vision; c Steve Stone; bl Shutterstock/Nick Paviakis; br Shutterstock/Paul Picone; back cover Shutterstock/Tramont_ana;
Page 4tl Photolibrary/Flirt Collection; 4br Photolibrary/Robert Harding; 5b Shutterstock/markrhiggins; 6cl Art Archive (AA)/Heraklion Archaeological Museum, Crete; 6br AA/Bibliothèque des Arts Décoratif;
7tr AKG/Heraklion Archaeological Museum, Crete; 8tc AA/National Archaeological Museum, Athens/Dagli Orti; 8tr AA/National Archaeological Museum, Athens/Dagli Orti; 9tl AA/National Archaeological
Museum, Athens/Dagli Orti; 9tr AA/National Archaeological Museum, Athens/Dagli Orti; 9br AA/National Archaeological Museum, Athens/Dagli Orti; 10bl AA/National Archaeological Museum, Athens/Dagli
Orti; 11tl AKG/Warner Bros./Alex Bailey; 11tr With the kind permission of the Trustees of the British Museum; 12tr AKG/British Museum; 15bl AKG/SMPK Antiquities Museum; 16tl AKG/Archives CDA/Guillo;
16bl iStockphoto; 17bc AKG/Erich Lessing; 18cl AKG/Erich Lessing; 18bl AKG/Narodowe Museum, Warsaw; 19t AA/Archaeological Museum, Sparta/Gianni Dagli Orti; 21tl Corbis/Gianni Dagli Orti; 22c
Shutterstock/James M. House; 22–23 Shutterstock/Maximmal; 23tl AKG/Erich Lessing; 23cr AA/Agora Museum, Athens/Gianni Dagli Orti; 23cl With the kind permission of the Trustees of the British Museum;
23br Getty/Time & Life Pictures; 23r Shutterstock/Alice; 24bl AKG/Musée du Louvre; 26–27 Art Archive/Bibliothèque des Arts Décoratifs, Paris/Dagli Orti; 26tr AA/Musée du Louvre/Dagli Orti; 26cl AKG/
Musée du Louvre; 27 iStockphoto; 28tl AA/Superstock; 28bc AA/Kanellopoulos Museum, Athens/Dagli Orti; 28r AKG/Kunsthistorisches Museum, Vienna; 29l Shutterstock/Denis Kornilov; 29tr With the
kind permission of the Trustees of the British Museum; 29cc AA/Agora Museum, Athens/Dagli Orti; 29cr AA/Soprintendenza Archaeologica, Salerno/Dagli Orti; 30tl Shutterstock/Panos Karapanagiotis;
30rc Shutterstock/RoxyFer; 30bl AKG/Erich Lessing; 30bc AA/Musée du Louvre; 30br AA/Musée du Louvre; 31tl Shutterstock/Oleg Seleznev; 31r Shutterstock/bumihills; 31bl Bridgeman Art Library/Ancient
Art & Architecture; 32tr AA/Kanellopoulos Museum, Athens/Dagli Orti; 32cl AA/Museo Nazionale Terme, Rome/Gianni Dagli Orti; 33tr AA/Museo di Villa Giulia, Rome/Gianni Dagli Orti; 33cr Shutterstock/
Evangelos; 34tl AA/Archaeological Museum, Istanbul/ Dagli Orti; 34tr AKG/Erich Lessing; 35tl AKG/Erich Lessing; 36br PA/AP; 37tl AKG/British Library; 37tr AA/Museo Nazionale Romano, Rome/Dagli Orti;
37cl AA/National Archaeological Museum, Athens/Gianni Dagli Orti; 37br AKG/North Wind Archives; 38–39 AA/ Musée Archéologique, Naples/Alfredo Dagli Orti; 38br Kobal/Warner Bros./Jaap Buitendijk;
39tr AKG/Bildarchiv Steffens; 40bl AKG/Erich Lessing; 41cr Kingfisher/Steve Weston; 41br Getty/Lonely Planet; 42tl Marie-Lan Nguy; 42b Photolibrary/Waterframe; 43tl AKG/Nimatallah; 43cr Album/Oronoz;
43br PA/AP; 48tr AA/Museo Nazionale Reggio, Calabria/Dagli Orti; 48cl Photolibrary/P. Narayan; 48cr Kobal/Warner Bros./Jaap Buitendijk; 48bl Shutterstock/Jozef Sedmak

CONTENTS

ILLYRIA

MACEDONIA

gold coin of Philip II
of Macedon showing
the hero Hercules

THRACE

About 80 percent
of the Greek
mainland is taken
up by mountains
and hills.

EPIRUS

CHALCIDICE

AEGEAN SEA

Mount Olympus,
home of the gods

MOUNT OLYMPUS

CORFU

PINDUS MOUNTAINS

THESSALY

GREECE   CYNOSCEPHALAE •

AETOLIA

THERMOPYLAE •

EUBOEA

LOCRIS   DELPHI •

PHOCIS
• ORCHOMENUS

• CHALCIS
• ERETRIA

BOEOTIA
• PLATAEA   • THEBES

ATTICA   • MARATHON

ACHAEA

Delphi, a major
religious site

MEGARA • SALAMIS •   • ATHENS
• PIRAEUS

• ELIS

CORINTH •
NEMEA •
MYCENAE •
ARGOS •   • TIRYNS   • EPIDAURUS

OLYMPIA •

PELOPONNESE

Parthenon, a temple that
overlooks the city of
Athens, the most powerful
state in Greece, c. 400s B.C.

ANCIENT CIVILIZATIONS

Ruined cities, temples, and theaters can
still be seen in Greece. Most date from
the great age of the Greek city-states,
between the 700s and 300s B.C. The
civilizations that flourished in Greece
between 5,000 and 2,300 years ago still
affect the way we see the world today.

MESSENIA

statue of Zeus
at Olympia,
c. 432 B.C.

• PYLOS

• SPARTA

LACONIA

Sparta, a
military state

IONIAN SEA

VOYAGE
TO GREECE

Greece can be visited by ship, crossing the dark blue
waters of the Aegean or Ionian seas. Island after island
appears on the horizon. Beyond them lies the Greek
mainland, where mountains and rocky shores surround
plains and groves of olive trees. The climate is hot and
dry in the summer but mild and moist in the winter. In
ancient times, this beautiful, sunny land was called Hellas.

ACROSS THE WAVES

These fish and dolphins were painted
at the palace of Knossos on the island
of Crete more than 3,500 years ago.
Greece is a land of coasts and islands.
Its seas were sailed by fishermen,
merchants, pirates, and warriors.

MEDITERRANEAN
SEA

Earthquakes are common in Greece. They were said to be the work of the god Poseidon (see page 14).

BLACK SEA

BYZANTIUM •

The Bosphorus Strait divides Europe from Asia.

SEA OF MARMARA

PHRYGIA

• TROY

Greek soldiers were said to have hidden inside a wooden horse to gain access to the city of Troy.

LESBOS

MYSIA

ASIA MINOR

• PHOCAEA

CHIOS

• SMYRNA

LYDIA

AEGEAN SEA

• EPHESUS

SAMOS

• PRIENE

DELOS

IONIA

CARIA

CYCLADES

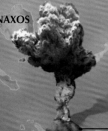

NAXOS

• HALICARNASSUS

LYCIA

LANDS OF THE GREEKS

The Greek mainland forms part of the Balkan peninsula, in southern Europe. Its ragged coastline breaks up into headlands, inlets, and chains of islands. These divide the eastern Mediterranean into a number of smaller seas, straits, and gulfs. In ancient times, Greeks also settled along the coasts of Asia Minor, or Anatolia (in modern Turkey).

KEY

religious place

site of a battle

THERA
(SANTORINI)

massive volcanic eruption on Santorini, c. 1600 B.C.

RHODES

"FUTURE AGES WILL WONDER AT US, AS THE PRESENT AGE WONDERS AT US NOW."

words of the Athenian leader Pericles
as reported by the historian Thucydides (c. 460–395 B.C.)

SEA OF CRETE

Minoan palace of Knossos, c. 1700–1350 B.C.

KNOSSOS

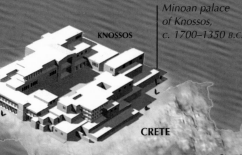

CRETE

⊖ THE GREEK SPIRIT

For most of its history, Greece was not united as a single nation. Instead, it was made up of rival cities and small city-states. Sometimes, these joined forces, but often they fought against one another. Even so, throughout most of their history, all Greeks shared similar ways of life and the same language, view of the world, and religious practices.

Greek horsemen ride through Athens.

PEOPLE OF THE PALACE

Crete is the largest island in Greece. It has high mountains and is surrounded by a sparkling, blue sea. It was here that Europe's first great civilization grew, between about 2700 and 1420 B.C. Its people worked with metals and traded with the rest of Europe, Egypt, and Asia. The legendary ruler of Crete was named Minos, so this civilization is often called "Minoan."

THE BULLS OF KNOSSOS

It was daring, death defying, and acrobatic! Young men, and probably young women, too, would vault over the horns of a bull and perform flips. Bulls were sacred in Crete, so this sport was probably part of a religious ritual watched by the royal court in Knossos.

PRINCE OF THE LILIES

Beautiful wall paintings have been found at Knossos, the site of a splendid palace. They show lords and ladies, flowers, birds, and dolphins. Fine Minoan paintings have also been found on the nearby island of Thera (Santorini), which was destroyed by a massive volcanic eruption about 3,600 years ago.

CRETE'S DARK SECRET

Ancient myths tell of a savage monster called the Minotaur, who was half man and half bull. He was imprisoned in the Labyrinth, a maze built by a cunning engineer named Daedalus. Eventually, the hero Theseus, who founded the city of Athens, discovered a way through the maze and killed the monster (right).

An acrobat waits to catch the bull leaper.

> The eruption of Thera may have triggered a tsunami—a huge ocean wave—that devastated the coast of Crete.

Vaults and somersaults require perfect timing.

THE DOUBLE AX

Goddesses were more significant than gods in the Minoan religion. They are sometimes shown with an ax called a *labrys*, which may have been used to sacrifice bulls. Small, ornamental axes were used as amulets, or charms.

The *labrys* had twin blades.

Cretan bulls have long, sharp horns.

LORDS OF THE CITADEL

CITADEL—a stronghold or fortress defending a settlement or city

On rocks above the plains of mainland Greece, royal halls and new settlements began to appear. They were the homes of kings, queens, and warrior groups. Fortified citadels with strong stone walls have been discovered at Tiryns, Thebes, Pylos, Athens, Orchomenus, and Mycenae. We call this civilization "Mycenaean." From about 1600 B.C., the Mycenaeans became ever more powerful. They eventually conquered Minoan Crete.

bronze dagger blades inlaid with gold, from Mycenae, 1500s B.C.

gold-handled dagger from Pylos, 1500s B.C.

THE WARRIORS

Mycenaean warriors fought with swords, daggers, and long spears. They wore bronze armor and bore large shields covered in ox hides. Chariots carried them to battle.

two lionesses carved in stone above the gate

> A myth claimed that the walls of Mycenae and Tiryns were built by one-eyed giants known as the Cyclopes.

A CUP FOR A KING

The Mycenaeans often used Minoan goldsmiths. This gold cup features a picture of a bull. It was found at Vapheio, near Sparta in southern Greece, and was made between 1500 and 1400 B.C.

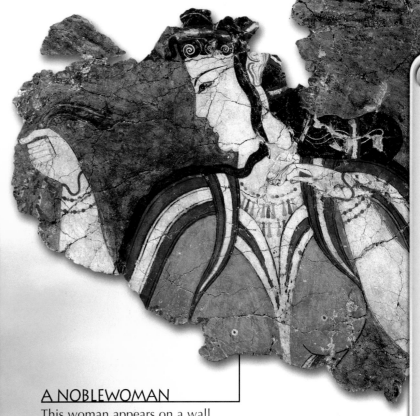

THROUGH THE LION GATE

The citadel of Mycenae overlooked the Argive plain, 55 mi. (90km) to the west of Athens. Its 3,000-ft. (900-m)-long walls were made of huge, strong stone blocks, some of them weighing as much as 13 tons. The walls would have been up to 40 ft. (12m) high and 23 ft. (7m) thick. The Lion Gate was the entrance to the palace within the walls. A town spread across the lower slopes, outside the fortification.

A NOBLEWOMAN

This woman appears on a wall painting from Mycenae. She dates from the 1200s B.C. and wears rich clothes and jewelry. Mycenaean nobles were wealthy and enjoyed perfumes, fine pottery, linen and woolen textiles, and tiled floors.

The main gates were defended by extended walls called bastions.

⊜ MASK OF GOLD

This magnificent gold mask was placed over the face of a man who was buried in the graves of Mycenae. It was discovered in 1876 by a famous German archaeologist named Heinrich Schliemann. He thought that he had found the remains of a legendary Greek king named Agamemnon, but the mask dates from 1550 to 1500 B.C., centuries before the time when Agamemnon was believed to have ruled.

so-called Mask of Agamemnon

Battle chariots are pulled by two horses.

The Trojan citadel is set on fire by the enemy.

Long, bronze swords are used for hand-to-hand fighting.

A Mycenaean champion engages in combat.

WAR WITH TROY

Mycenaean warriors sailed to attack islands and coasts around the Aegean Sea. They wore helmets made of boars' tusks and fought fiercely with bronze weapons. They attacked fortified cities such as Troy, in what is now Turkey. For hundreds of years, Greeks liked to tell exciting tales about their battles with Troy. These may have been based on many different conflicts or possibly on one great "Trojan War" in the 1190s and 1180s B.C.

COLLAPSE OF THE PALACES

The Mycenaean age came to an end around 1200 B.C. when the great palaces were destroyed. Clay tablets, written in a script called Linear B, survive from some of the palaces and tell us about the Mycenaeans and their society.

 > Greeks told of how the Trojan War started when Helen, a beautiful queen, was carried off by Paris, prince of Troy.

www.bbc.co.uk/schools/troy

WOODEN HORSE

This scene is from the movie *Troy* (2004), which is based on a story from the *Iliad* (see panel, right). A huge wooden horse is shown being pulled into the Trojan citadel. Greek soldiers were hiding inside the horse. They tricked the Trojans into defeat.

HOMER'S HEROES

Deadly combat, treachery, bravery, love, and fate all play a part in one of the most famous tales ever told, the *Iliad*. Its stirring poetry imagines a time late in the Trojan War and describes, in detail, great battles of Greek and Trojan warriors. The *Iliad* was probably written soon after 700 B.C., but it was based on songs handed down by generations of skilled poets. Did these songs include memories that reached back to Mycenaean times?

the *Iliad*'s Greek hero, Achilles (left), in battle

GREEKS VERSUS TROJANS

For many years, scholars believed that accounts of the Trojan War were no more than stories. Then, between 1871 and 1890, the German archaeologist Heinrich Schliemann discovered the remains of the city of Troy near Hisarlik in Turkey. We now know that this site was occupied for thousands of years—and shows evidence of destruction in about 1180 B.C.

"HECTOR LEAPED TO THE GROUND FROM HIS CHARIOT FULLY ARMED . . . DRIVING HIS FIGHTERS INTO BATTLE."

Homer
earliest Greek poet, from the Iliad *(c. 680 B.C.)*

The Myceneans' long spears protect the front rank. They are not thrown.

⊕ THE VOYAGES OF ODYSSEUS

What happened after the Trojan War? Homer's *Odyssey* tells the story of a warrior king named Odysseus, whose journey home to Ithaca takes ten long years. This is an exciting tale about gods, goddesses, monsters, and bird-women called Sirens, who lure sailors to death with their singing. We are told of shipwrecks, magic, and revenge. At the time these stories were written, after 700 B.C., many Greeks were already seafaring far from home.

Odysseus and the Sirens

Colonists sail in search of new lands.

Greek islands

SEAS AND CITIES

The citadels of the Mycenaeans lay in ruins after centuries of war. In their place, new communities appeared. Iron, which was harder and tougher than bronze, was being hammered into weapons and tools. Greece became a patchwork of small states. These were based on islands or on a single city and its surrounding land. Each city-state (called a *polis*) was independent. Famous city-states included Athens, Sparta, Thebes, and Corinth.

CARGOES AND TRADE

Greek merchants, known as *emporoi*, shipped wheat, timber, marble, silver, and pottery. Wine and olive oil were transported in pottery jars called *amphorae*.

amphorae

Sailors carry cargo on board.

> Colonists took fire from the mother city to start their first fire in the new colony.

THE WIDER WORLD

Many Greek city-states were surrounded by mountains or rocky coasts, with poor soil for farming. Groups of settlers went out in search of better land to build new communities. These overseas colonies were independent but kept strong links with their "mother city" (or *metropolis*). Greeks settled around the Black Sea and in Asia Minor, North Africa, Italy, France, and Spain. Some of Europe's best-known cities, including Naples in Italy and Marseille in France, were Greek colonies.

A GREEK CITY

This Greek city is built by the coast on a steep hillside. It has a busy harbor for fishing boats and merchant ships. A road leads from the marketplace and houses to a high rock, where there is a temple built of marble.

www.ancientgreece.co.uk/geography/home_set.html

ACROSS THE WAVES

This wooden merchant ship uses oars as well as a large, square sail. It is steered by one man, with a long side oar near the stern.

naukleros, or
ship owner

Hephaestus
*god of fire,
blacksmiths, and forges*

Aphrodite
*goddess of love
and beauty, whose
symbol was a dove*

Dionysus
*god of wine and drama,
who was worshiped
at wild festivals*

Ares
*god of war and
a bloodthirsty warrior,
whose father was Zeus*

Hera
*wife of Zeus and queen
of the gods, who was also
the goddess of marriage*

Poseidon
*god of the sea,
earthquakes, and horses,
often shown holding a trident*

GODS OF OLYMPUS

Early Greek stories told how the universe was created from chaos. Out of this the first gods and goddesses came into being, representing the earth, the sea, the sky, and night and day. The Greeks had tales about many other gods, too. These represented human feelings such as love, forces of nature such as earthquakes, or human activities such as farming or fighting. Stories of giants, monsters, spirits, and heroes were also told.

**peaks of
Mount Olympus**

POWER AND FATE

The most important gods and goddesses were said to live on the snowy summit of Greece's highest mountain, Olympus. They were ruled by Zeus, the god of the sky, and were like humans, forever arguing among themselves. The gods and goddesses controlled the fate of human beings—they punished them, rewarded them, bewitched them, and sometimes even fell in love with them.

"THEN WE WENT TO THE GOD'S PRECINCT, AND THERE ON THE ALTAR OUR CAKES AND OFFERINGS WERE DEDICATED, FOOD FOR HEPHAESTUS' FLAME."

Aristophanes (c. 448–388 B.C.)
Greek poet, from his play Wealth *(c. 388 B.C.)*

 ❯ One myth tells that Athena was so jealous of Arachne the weaver's skills that she turned her into a spider.

http://greece.mrdonn.org/greekgods/index.html

Zeus
king of the gods, god of the sky, and the commander of thunder and lightning

Apollo
god of light, who was also linked with music, poetry, and archery

Demeter
mother goddess representing fertility, farming, and the seasons

Athena
patron goddess of Athens, victorious in battle, and worshiped for her wisdom

Hermes
messenger of the gods, who was worshiped by businessmen—and thieves!

Artemis
moon goddess and a huntress with a bow and arrow

⊖ THE ORACLE AT DELPHI

Delphi was a religious site on the slopes of Mount Parnassus. It was sacred to Apollo, who killed Python, a snake goddess who guarded the earth. Delphi was famous for its oracle. A priestess would go into a trance and speak the words of Apollo. Rulers and the famous would visit Delphi for guidance about their futures.

TO THE TEMPLE

Greeks made offerings to the gods at their temples. Each year there would be a public procession to the temple in honor of a god or goddess, bringing an animal such as a sheep for sacrifice. At least one priest would have accompanied the procession on its journey.

consulting the oracle (priestess is seated on the left)

⊙ TO VICTORY

Warriors and chariots decorate the rim of this bronze krater, a vase used for mixing wine and water. It was made in Laconia around 530 B.C. but was found far away in France. Bronze work was a key export from Laconia.

design celebrating the victory of warriors

shield (hoplon) made of bronze, wood, and leather

stabbing spear, 6.5–10 ft. (2–3m) long

helmet with horsehair crest

THE SNARLING FOX

A Spartan boy once stole a fox. He hid it beneath his cloak. When challenged, he refused to admit the truth, even though the fox was gnawing and biting him. He died of his wounds. The Spartans saw no shame in stealing, only in being found out.

FIGHTING FIT

In Sparta, the physically weak might be killed at birth. From an early age, Spartan boys were trained in physical exercise, wrestling, and combat. Cowards ("tremblers") were despised.

learning how to wrestle

> HOPLITE—an armed foot soldier in ancient Greece

bronze greave (shin guard) to protect the lower leg

SHIELDS OF SPARTA

Who needs stone walls around their city if they have the bravest warriors? That was the proud boast of the city-state of Sparta. The Spartans were definitely the toughest fighters in Greece. They conquered the regions of Laconia and Messenia in the south by about 550 B.C. and forced the local people to work for them as laborers called "helots." This left the Spartans free—to train for war.

THE RED CLOAKS

At the age of seven, Spartan boys were taken from their parents and sent to live in a barracks with other boys of the same age. The discipline was very harsh. From the age of 20, a male could wear the famous red cloak of a Spartan warrior, or hoplite (literally meaning "shield bearer"). A hoplite could be called up to fight at any time until he reached the age of 60. Their armor was expensive, and each hoplite had to buy his own. Dead hoplites were carried from the battlefield on their shields.

SPARTAN GIRLS

Girls in Sparta were taught to race and wrestle. Most Greeks were shocked by this. Elsewhere, young women were expected to stay inside their house, spin and weave wool, and give birth to children.

> The Spartans were ruled by two kings at the same time.

www.sparta.net and www.ancientgreece.co.uk/sparta/home_set.html

THE IMMORTALS

Xerxes' Persian army, perhaps 250,000 strong, was led by elite troops (left) known as the Immortals. As the Spartan king Leonidas marched north, he gained the support of only a few thousand hoplites from other Greek states. No large army followed after him.

TO THERMOPYLAE

By the summer of 480 B.C., the Persians were approaching Thermopylae, a narrow pass between the seashore and mountains in central Greece. An advance group of 300 Spartan hoplites rushed north. Their job seemed impossible—to hold back or delay the Persian advance.

Greek hoplite attacking Persian cavalry

Wave after wave of Persians attack the Greek line.

> EMPIRE—*many different lands brought together under a single ruler*

BATTLE IN THE PASS

About 2,500 years ago, Persia ruled the world's biggest empire. It stretched from Egypt to India and included Greek colonies in Asia Minor. These eastern Greeks revolted in 499 B.C., starting a war. A Persian invasion of the Greek mainland failed in 490 B.C., but in 481 B.C., a new Persian king named Xerxes decided to seek revenge. He assembled a huge army and fleet. Its mission was the conquest of all of Greece, by land and sea.

> "GO, STRANGER, AND TELL THEM IN SPARTA THAT WE LIE HERE, OBEDIENT TO THEIR COMMANDS."
>
> **Simonides (c. 556—468 B.C.)**
> *Greek poet, his lines in memory of the Spartans who died at Thermopylae*

The Spartans held the pass until the third day.

FIGHTING IN THE SHADE

The Spartans showed no fear. A local man warned that the Persians had so many archers that their arrows would block the sun. A hoplite named Dieneces laughed and said, "Good! Then we'll be fighting in the shade!" Throughout the first day of battle, wave after wave of Persian troops, even Immortals, fell to Spartan spears. At the end of the second day, Leonidas still held the pass, even though no Greek reinforcements had arrived.

bust of King Leonidas I of Sparta, who died in 480 B.C.

THE LAST STAND

In the end, the Persians bribed a local Greek to show them a secret path through the mountains. On the third day, Leonidas was attacked by Persians from all sides. Most other troops went home, but some Greek allies stayed to fight. It took the Greeks another year to finally beat the Persians, on another battlefield—Plataea.

> We still use the word *laconic* (meaning "Spartan") to describe someone who uses few words.

SHIPS AT WAR

Two long sweeps (steering oars) are operated by a helmsman at the stern.

TRIREME—a warship with three banks of oars

After 490 B.C., the city-state of Athens built a large navy. Soon it ruled the waves. Hundreds of warships could dock in Piraeus, the city's seaport. The fastest type of ship was the trireme, which used oar power to ram and sink the enemy. It had a mast with a single, square sail, but in battle, the deck was stripped bare for action.

A double flute called an aulos is blown to help the oarsmen keep time. The crew sing as they row into battle.

THREE BANKS OF OARS

Trireme (in Greek *trieres*) means a "three-oar" ship. The rowers were seated on staggered benches on three levels. Each oar was 13–13.8 ft. (4–4.2m) long.

 > The Delphic oracle predicted that Athens would be saved by its "wooden walls." The Athenians said that this meant its ships.

SEND IN THE MARINES

On the twin runways of the deck there was a group of up to 20 marines, or *epibatai*, including archers and armed hoplites for boarding enemy ships. The working crew of sailors numbered about 15.

MUSCLE POWER

Each ship needed 170 rowers, one for each oar. They were not slaves but professional sailors, mostly from poorer households. The top speed was about 8 knots (9 mph or 15km/h).

BATTLE OF SALAMIS

After the Battle of Thermopylae in 480 B.C., the Persians were poised to conquer Greece. Athens was in flames. However, 21 western Greek city-states raised a fleet of 378 ships. The huge Persian fleet included Phoenicians, Egyptians, and eastern Greeks, all from lands ruled by Persia. The western Greeks trapped the enemy in a channel near the island of Salamis. The battle lasted eight hours, and 200 Persian ships were destroyed.

A trireme fatally rams an enemy ship so that it is holed at the water line. Its rowers are thrown into the water on impact.

Persian ship

Athenian ships

"IMMEDIATELY SHIP STRUCK INTO SHIP ITS BRONZE-TIPPED PROW."
Aeschylus (c. 525–456 B.C.)

Greek dramatist, who served at Salamis, describes the battle in his play The Persians *(472 B.C.)*

The ram is a strong timber beam plated with bronze. It smashes into enemy ships.

DEMOCRACY—a state governed by its citizens or by their representatives

ATHENS IN ITS GLORY

During the 400s B.C., Athens experienced a golden age. Its large fleet of warships made it the most powerful of all of the Greek city-states. Athens benefited from the Attica region's rich silver mines and grew wealthy through trade. The city became an exciting center of discussion and new ideas— of philosophy, politics, drama, writing, sculpture, architecture, and fine craft skills.

THE GODDESS CITY

Athens was built around a high, rocky stronghold, or Acropolis. On top of this was the Parthenon, a great temple to the goddess Athena, who protected the city. It housed a statue of ivory and gold, almost 43 ft. (13m) high. The city spread out below, a sea of tiled roofs and white walls. There were houses and courtyards, law courts, and market halls. About 250,000 people may have lived in Athens and the surrounding region.

The Parthenon was a temple made from white marble. This rich stone displayed the wealth of the city.

> It was said that the goddess Athena created the olive tree as a gift for the city of Athens.

www.bbc.co.uk/schools/primaryhistory/ancient_greeks/athens

SILVER OWL

Athenians minted silver coins. This one shows an owl, the emblem of Athena, the goddess of wisdom. Owl coins were traded for goods throughout the ancient world.

◉ PEOPLE POWER

Our word *politics* comes from *polis*, Greek for "city-state." Athens was the first state to attempt to be ruled by its own people. This system was called *demokratía*, or democracy. All citizens could attend the assembly to make political decisions. Court cases were decided by juries of hundreds of citizens. But women and slaves were excluded from the democracy.

jurors' tickets used in the *dikasterion* (law court) in Athens, 300s B.C.

"OUR CONSTITUTION IS NAMED A DEMOCRACY, BECAUSE IT IS IN THE HANDS NOT OF THE FEW BUT OF THE MANY."

Thucydides (c. 460–400 B.C.)
Athenian politician and historian, from his
History of the Peloponnesian War, Book 1 *(431 B.C.)*

THE AGE OF PERICLES

Pericles lived from about 495 to 429 B.C. He was a great Athenian statesman, an excellent public speaker, and a military leader who also encouraged the arts and the creation of beautiful architecture.

RIVAL POWERS

After the war with Persia, the Greek city-states formed a military alliance called the Delian League, controlled by Athens. Its power was challenged by the Peloponnesian League, led by Sparta. From 431 to 404 B.C., Greek fought against Greek by land and sea.

DAILY LIFE

▽ AGORA—a district serving as the center of public life in a Greek town

Older Greek towns developed around a maze of streets and alleys. Later cities were better planned. Around a town you might see women with pottery jars collecting the daily water supply from street fountains or wells, slaves loading donkeys with supplies, or children playing in the dust. The agora was the main meeting place. This was where men came to do business or talk politics and where traders came to sell their goods.

⊖ GREEK CHILDHOOD

Many babies died at birth. Those who survived were given their names after a week or so. Athenian boys might be taught their father's trade or go to school to learn reading, writing, arithmetic, music, and gymnastics. Girls might learn at home, studying reading, writing, music, and weaving. At about age 12, children were expected to give their toys to the gods as a sign that they were grown up.

child taking a toy to an altar, c. 425 B.C.

THE WOMEN'S ROOM

Women got married when they were about 15 years old. They spent many hours each week spinning yarn and weaving cloth. In this room they might also play music, nurse their children, or eat their meals.

bedroom

kitchen

bathroom

ENSLAVED

There may have been as many slaves as free citizens in ancient Greece. They had to work as servants, nurses, cooks, laborers, or miners. Some were born into slavery or sold as slaves during childhood. Others had been captured in wars.

❯ In Greece, a home break-in was exactly that. Burglars could easily smash through the mud-brick walls.

Woolen blankets, clothes, and wall hangings were woven on upright looms.

slaves' quarters

women's room

INSIDE THE HOME

Most homes were built of mud bricks and plaster and had stone foundations and tiled roofs. Windows were small with wooden shutters. Wives managed the household and spent much of their time in the women's room. They had few rights, although in Sparta they could own property. Men led more public lives. Their room was used for business meetings or for entertaining friends.

www.ancientgreece.co.uk/dailylife/challenge/cha_set.html

men's room

bedroom

entrance hall

couches laid out for a symposium (a drinking and discussion party)

playing knucklebones

storeroom

courtyard

juggling

workshop

THE COURTYARD

In the courtyard, slaves might be carrying in the shopping or sweeping up. Children would be playing or having lessons under a shady olive tree. Also, cooking or eating might take place here on sunny days.

PLAYTIME

Games included juggling (above) and knucklebones, in which five small bones or stones were tossed, caught, and flipped on the hand. Small children played with dolls, toy animals, wheeled carts, and yo-yos.

FEEDING THE PEOPLE

Greek farmers grew olive trees and grape vines and raised sheep, goats, pigs, geese, and chickens. Fields were plowed with oxen, and hardy crops of barley—or wheat in the more fertile valleys— were harvested with sickles each July. Summers were hot and dusty. Farmers built stone terraces across their rocky land to stop the soil from being blown away by the wind or washed away by the rain.

SYMPOSIUM—a party for men, with eating, drinking, discussion, and entertainment

HUNTING AND FISHING
This picture shows a famous boar hunt from Greek mythology. The countryside offered plenty of animals for hunting, including wild boar, deer, and hares. Thrushes and doves were trapped for food, and fish and octopuses were netted or speared along the coasts.

STIR IT UP
A woman uses a long ladle to stir a cauldron of stew as it simmers over the fire. At home, a kitchen oven was used for baking, and a portable brazier was used for outdoor cooking in the courtyard (see page 25).

Symposium guests reclined as they ate and drank.

> Poorer men ate and drank cheap wine at taverns called *kapeleia* rather than host an expensive symposium.

SEAFOOD AND WINE

Breakfast in ancient Greece might have been little more than a barley cake or a bowl of oatmeal, and lunch was a simple crust of bread, goat's cheese, figs, or an egg. The evening meal was more substantial, perhaps with beans, lentils, onions, chicken, sausage or seafood, and pears or pomegranates. While women ate in their own rooms, wealthy men and their guests would eat in theirs. A male party, or symposium, included a lot of wine drinking. There might be serious discussions and arguments or entertainment with dancers and drinking games.

olive oil

herbs

onions

wheat

cheese

beans

grapes

fish

eggs

shellfish

figs

honey

IN THE KITCHEN

Olive oil was stored in jars. Certain meats were often eaten as part of religious rituals, but fish could be bought at any market and was preserved by salting or drying it. Wild herbs and garlic added flavor, and honey was used to sweeten cakes. Vegetables and fruit were eaten in season, making for a healthy diet.

Strong wine was mixed with water and drunk from a kylix (a wide, shallow cup).

LINEN—a smooth, cool textile made from a plant called Flax

HAIR FASHION

Greek women had long, flowing hair. In Sparta, hair was tied back in a ponytail, but in Athens, hair was braided into a bun with ribbons. Later fashions tucked curled hair into bands, nets, and beautiful headdresses. Wigs and hair extensions were popular.

RIBBONS AND ROBES

Most Greek clothes were beautiful but simple. They were woven on looms at home and were usually made from high-quality wool or linen. White cloth was popular, but bold colors could also be produced using natural dyes made from plants, insects, and shellfish. By the 400s B.C., expensive silks and cottons were being imported from China and India.

The tunic falls in natural folds.

THE LOOK

Mirrors were made of polished bronze. What did they reflect? Rich women used makeup such as eyeliner and blush and powder to make their faces pale. They did not want to look like poor women, who became sunburned working in the fields.

DRAPES AND FOLDS

This woman wears a peplos tunic. She has draped an outer wrap from her shoulder pin around her hips. Outer wraps were called himatia and could also be worn to veil the head or act as a cloak.

Face powder was made from lead and was, in fact, poisonous.

WHAT TO WEAR

Greek dress was based on a tunic design made from a single piece of cloth. Tunics were knee length for working people or slaves and ankle length for wealthier citizens. The classic dress for women was a peplos—a sleeveless tunic with a high belt. It was pinned at each shoulder. Various styles of chiton also came into fashion. These were lighter, looser tunics, often with sleeves. Men also wore a simple version of the chiton.

To stay cool, the himation is draped low.

necklace
c. 450 B.C.

earrings
c. 850 B.C.

gold ring
c. 450 B.C.

MENSWEAR

This man wears no undertunic, or chiton, but just a large wrap, or himation. This was much like the toga worn by Roman men. Men would often wear no clothes at all for exercising or military training.

GLEAMING GOLD

Gold, silver, ivory, and precious stones were made into beautiful earrings, headdresses, pendants, necklaces, and rings. These were often expensive gifts and brought out only on special occasions. Rings were sometimes worn as lucky charms or in honor of the gods.

● OUT AND ABOUT

Greeks often went barefoot, especially at home. The normal footwear was a pair of sandals made of leather thongs. Short or high boots could be worn for riding horses or working outdoors. During hot Mediterranean summers, a broad, brimmed straw hat was ideal. On cooler, more wintry days, a cap or a fur hat might be needed, as well as a warm, woolen cloak.

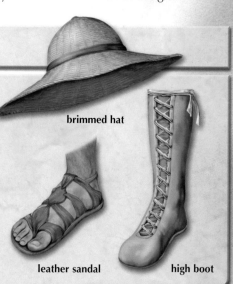

brimmed hat

leather sandal

high boot

www.metmuseum.org/toah/hd/grdr/hd_grdr.htm

MARBLE—a type of rock, often white in color, used to make statues and buildings

capital

pillar

Doric
*fluted (lined)
column with a plain,
simple capital*

Ionic
*capital (top)
is carved with
graceful scroll*

CARVED COLUMNS

The Greeks were masters of arts
and crafts, producing objects
with technical skill and a sense
of beauty. Magnificent public
buildings and temples were
supported by tall pillars, designed
in various styles called "orders."
Their tops, or capitals, were
beautifully carved. Greek
architecture, with its perfect
proportions, would be imitated
for thousands of years.

CREATING BEAUTY

Greek cities were noisy, industrious places.
Around the agora, the central market, were
busy workshops where blacksmiths
hammered iron and bronze, silversmiths made
jewelry, and stoneworkers chiseled blocks of
marble. Potters produced fine vases, decorated
at first with geometric patterns and later with
figures of people or gods in black and red.
Some goods were made on a large scale and
exported around the Mediterranean.

⊜ THE POTTER'S CRAFT

Many Greek city-states had access to good clay. This sticky
mud was used to make urns, vases, jugs, pitchers, and jars.
These objects were generally shaped on a potter's wheel and
fired (baked) in a kiln until hard. During the firing, the amount
of air could be varied, which made the clay turn red. Areas
painted with a coating, called a slip, remained black.

geometrical ware
*patterned jug with
a decorative spout,
c. 675–650 B.C.*

red figure ware
*shows a scene from
the Trojan War,
c. 480 B.C.*

black figure ware
*cup featuring a bird catcher
from Etruria (an area of
central Italy), c. 550 B.C.*

> Archaeologists have discovered that many marble statues were originally colored with paints.

Corinthian
*slender column
is topped with ornate
stone leaves*

**Statues of women, called
caryatids, served as
pillars at the fronts of
some buildings.**

LIVING MARBLE

Greek sculptors worked in marble, bronze, and clay.
The first statues looked rather stiff and unnatural.
After the A.D. 500s, the human body was shown in a
much more realistic way for the first time in history.

HOT METAL

Blacksmiths used furnaces to heat iron. They created
the heat by puffing in air using leather bellows. Then
they shaped the soft metal into tools and weapons. Other
specialists worked precious ornamental metals such as
gold, silver, and electrum (a mixture of the two metals).

"BEAUTY IS TRUTH, TRUTH BEAUTY."

John Keats (1795–1821)

English poet, from his poem "Ode on a Grecian Urn" (1819)

THE OLYMPIC GAMES

PENTATHLON—a five-event athletic contest

"LIVE BY RULE, SUBMIT TO DIET ... EXERCISE YOUR BODY AT STATED HOURS, IN HEAT OR IN COLD ..."

Epictetus (A.D. 55–135)
philosopher, his words on training for the Olympics, from **The Enchiridion** *(A.D. 135)*

Thrilling athletic contests, or games, were held in Delphi, Nemea, Corinth, and Olympia and were open to athletes from all over the Greek world. The games began as a kind of religious festival, held in honor of the gods. The Olympic Games are believed to have started in 776 B.C. and were celebrated every four years until A.D. 393. They were revived as an international competition in 1896 and have become the biggest sporting event of the modern world.

statue of Zeus as Horkios, taker of oaths, with a lightning bolt in each hand

RUNNING FOR ZEUS

During the Olympic Games, city-states had to stop fighting one another. Nobody traveling to the games could be harmed, for they were under the special protection of the gods. Athletes and officials joined a two-day procession from Elis to Olympia—a valley in southwestern Greece—where there was a large temple dedicated to Zeus. There they were welcomed by an excited crowd. The Olympic site included other temples, tracks, racecourses, hostels, and restaurants.

TOP EVENTS

The footrace was originally the most important event in the games. The first known Olympic champion was Coroebus, a baker from Elis, in 776 B.C. Javelin, discus (left), running, and long jump were not separate events but were part of the pentathlon, which was decided by a wrestling match between the top two athletes.

Boars are sacrificed to Zeus, the king of the gods.

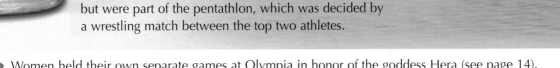

> Women held their own separate games at Olympia in honor of the goddess Hera (see page 14).

THRILLS AND SPILLS

More sports were added to the games, including boxing, running in armor, all-in combat, and horseracing. One of the most popular events was chariot racing, with teams of two or four horses. The action was fast and furious—and very dangerous for the charioteers.

The games begin with a swearing-in ceremony at the council chamber.

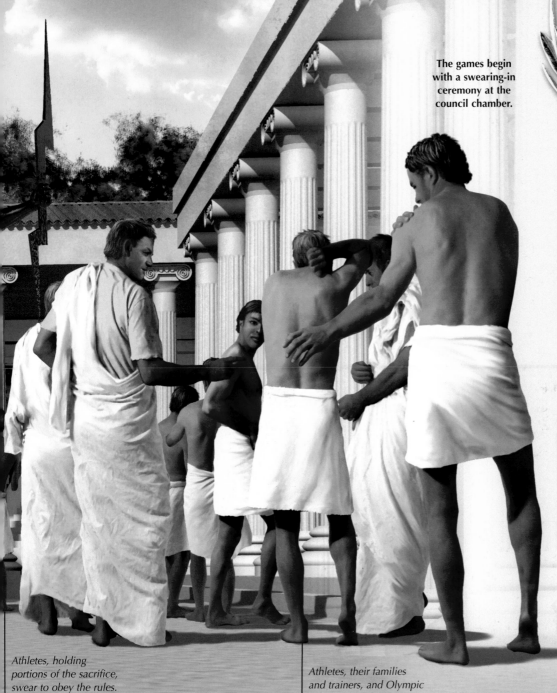

Athletes, holding portions of the sacrifice, swear to obey the rules.

Athletes, their families and trainers, and Olympic officials all line up to take the oath to Zeus.

THE CHAMPIONS

At the end of the games, the winners were summoned to the Temple of Zeus. They were not given medals but were crowned by the judges with a wreath of olive leaves. Finally, a great feast was held in their honor.

FAIR PLAY

Athletes were not supposed to be paid, but a winner could expect to be showered with gifts when he returned to his home city. Sometimes, there were political arguments and accusations of foul play. Fines imposed on cheats were used to pay for new statues of Zeus at Olympia.

▽ LYRE—a stringed musical instrument, originally with a tortoiseshell sound box

MASKS AND MUSIC

The Greeks loved words and the sound of words—poetry, music, and performing arts, such as dance and theater. All of these activities were closely linked and were said to be inspired by divine spirits called the Muses. The arts were powerfully connected to ancient religious rituals and festivals, but they were also rooted in the everyday life of villages and towns—and in fun and entertainment.

THE POET

Homer's poetry described wars and adventures. Later poets were more personal—praising nature or love or grieving for the dead. Poetry accompanied by the music of a lyre was called "lyric." One popular lyric poet was Sappho (above) from Lesbos.

THE DANCERS

Frenzied dancing was part of the worship of Dionysus, while stately dances to a lyre's music honored the god Apollo. There were dances for war, weddings, funerals, and entertainment.

theatron—where the audience sits to view the performance

Theaters are semicircular, with raised rows of stone benches.

TRAGEDY OR COMEDY?

Greek drama began as religious ritual and was a powerful creative force that soon took on a wider role in society. Greek dramatists of the 500s and 400s B.C., such as Aeschylus, Sophocles, Euripides, and Aristophanes, shaped our modern ideas of theater. They wrote sad, serious plays called tragedies, as well as funny plays called comedies. Actors performed in daylight in the open air, with seats in raised rows on which the audience watched the action on the stage.

THE CHORUS

In front of the stage, at least a dozen performers represented a group of characters—such as the women of a city—and sang or chanted together in verse. The chorus commented on the characters or explained the action of the play.

▷ Theater masks had funnel-shaped mouths that may have been used to amplify the voice (make it louder).

"OH THEBES ... OH CITY ...
COME DANCE THE
DANCE OF GOD!"

Euripides (c. 480–406 B.C.)
spoken by the chorus in his play Bacchae *(405 B.C.)*

*An actor playing a
god is lowered by
a crane and cable.*

MASKS

Actors wore exaggerated
masks to make them appear
larger than life. They showed
a character's age, sex, and
mood and made it easier
for one actor to play several
roles. Both male and female
parts were played by men.

⬤ MAKER OF SWEET MUSIC

Myths tell of a musician named
Orpheus, whose playing of the
lyre calmed wild beasts and
brought nature to a standstill.
People played music when
going into battle, at sporting
events, in religious processions,
and for private entertainment.
Instruments included the lyre
and *kithara*, as well as trumpets,
cymbals, flutes, double pipes
(*auloi*), pipes of Pan, and drums.

Orpheus playing his lyre

*The main action
of a tragedy is
staged here.*

*Slain heroes
are rolled onto
the stage.*

**skene—the building
behind the stage in
which the costumes
are stored**

*Costumes are
richly detailed and
brightly colored.*

*An altar to the god
Dionysus stands
in the orchestra.*

*The most important
people sit in the
front row.*

*Audiences
can number
15,000 or more.*

**orchestra—the
central area where
the chorus performs**

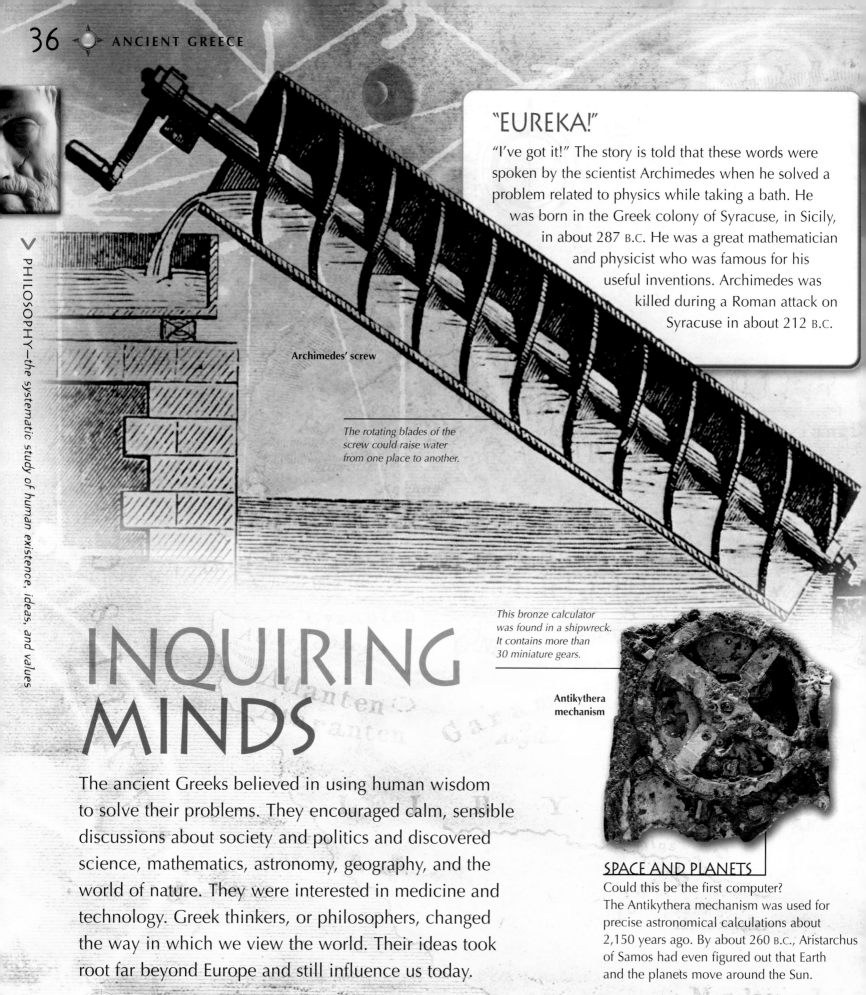

PHILOSOPHY—the systematic study of human existence, ideas, and values

Archimedes' screw

The rotating blades of the screw could raise water from one place to another.

"EUREKA!"

"I've got it!" The story is told that these words were spoken by the scientist Archimedes when he solved a problem related to physics while taking a bath. He was born in the Greek colony of Syracuse, in Sicily, in about 287 B.C. He was a great mathematician and physicist who was famous for his useful inventions. Archimedes was killed during a Roman attack on Syracuse in about 212 B.C.

This bronze calculator was found in a shipwreck. It contains more than 30 miniature gears.

Antikythera mechanism

INQUIRING MINDS

The ancient Greeks believed in using human wisdom to solve their problems. They encouraged calm, sensible discussions about society and politics and discovered science, mathematics, astronomy, geography, and the world of nature. They were interested in medicine and technology. Greek thinkers, or philosophers, changed the way in which we view the world. Their ideas took root far beyond Europe and still influence us today.

SPACE AND PLANETS

Could this be the first computer? The Antikythera mechanism was used for precise astronomical calculations about 2,150 years ago. By about 260 B.C., Aristarchus of Samos had even figured out that Earth and the planets move around the Sun.

> Eratosthenes (276–195 B.C.) may have estimated the distance around Earth to within one percent of the correct figure.

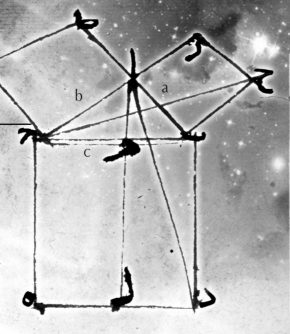

Pythagorean theorem:
$$a^2 + b^2 = c^2$$

b a

c

FIGURING IT OUT

The Greeks loved puzzling over problems of geometry—the mathematics of lines, angles, and area. At school, we still learn about the area of squares around a right triangle, a problem associated with Pythagoras (c. 570–495 B.C.). The greatest master of geometry was a genius named Euclid, who lived around 300 B.C.

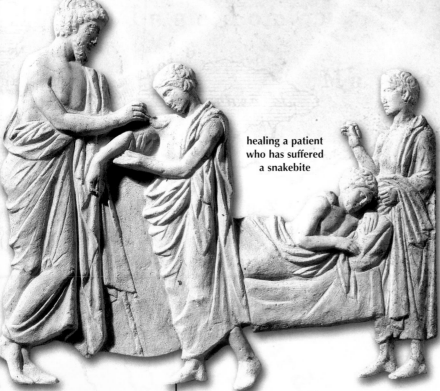

healing a patient who has suffered a snakebite

BRAINSTORMERS

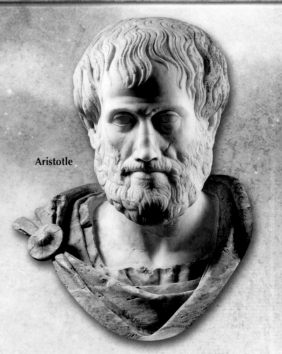

Aristotle

Philosophy means the "love of wisdom." Greek philosophers liked to argue about the natural world or how society should be organized. They asked questions about human behavior and what is right and wrong. Aristotle (384–322 B.C.) was one of the first great scientists. Socrates (c. 469–399 B.C.) was a philosopher who was put to death for spreading dangerous political ideas. Plato (c. 428–348 B.C.) founded the Academy in Athens, a center of philosophical debate.

www.ancientgreece.co.uk/knowledge/explore/exp_set.html

GREEK MEDICINE

Herbal cures and surgery took place at the shrines of Asclepius, the god of healing. Hippocrates of Kos (c. 460–370 B.C.) called for careful observation of patients and the study of their symptoms. Greek ideas about medicine were accepted in Europe and western Asia until the 1600s.

THE WIDER WORLD

As Greek sailors set out in search of new lands, geographers tried to make sense of the known world. The first one to try to draw a world map, with Greece at the center, was probably Anaximander (c. 610–546 B.C.). This map is based on the ideas of Hecataeus (550–476 B.C.).

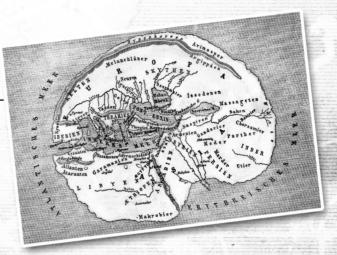

THE MARCH INTO ASIA

In 334 B.C., Alexander crossed into Asia with an army of 30,000 foot soldiers and 5,000 cavalry. Ahead were the troops of Darius III, the emperor of Persia. Alexander's men fought their way across Asia Minor and conquered the lands known today as Syria, Lebanon, Egypt, Iraq, Iran, parts of central Asia, and Afghanistan. Darius suffered bitter defeats at the Granicus River, at Issus, and Gaugamela. Alexander was victorious.

"O MY SON . . . MACEDONIA IS TOO SMALL FOR YOU."

King Philip II (382–336 B.C.)
said to his young son Alexander, as reported by the Greek historian Plutarch (c. A.D. 46–120)

ALEXANDER THE GREAT

King Alexander III was born in Pella, Macedonia, in 356 B.C. As a child, he was taught by the great philosopher Aristotle. In his short life, Alexander ("the Great") proved himself to be a brilliant general. He conquered one of the greatest empires the world had ever seen.

INDIAN WARFARE

In 326 B.C., Alexander reached the Hydaspes River—known today as the Jhelum, in Pakistan. He defeated an Indian army under King Puravura, who had 200 war elephants in his army.

THE AGE OF ALEXANDER

Macedonia was a kingdom on the northern borders of Greece. It became very powerful under the rule of a king named Philip II. In 338 B.C., Philip defeated an alliance of city-states, including Athens and Thebes, at the Battle of Chaeronea. He was murdered two years later. His son Alexander became king. Alexander put down rebellions and planned a war of all the Greeks against their old enemy, Persia.

> Alexander named a city in the Indus River valley after his favorite horse, Bucephalus.

DARIUS AT ISSUS

This mosaic picture, made in Italy in about 100 B.C., shows Alexander (below, left) fighting Darius (below), probably at the Battle of Issus in 333 B.C. Darius was killed by his own men in 330 B.C. Alexander gave him a fine funeral.

DEATH IN BABYLON

By 323 B.C., Alexander was in Babylon, in what is now Iraq. After a feast in the royal palace, he suffered a severe fever. Some people believed he had caught a disease such as malaria. Others thought he was poisoned by jealous rivals. He died at the age of only 32.

coins from the time of Alexander the Great

www.historyofmacedonia.org/AncientMacedonia/AlexandertheGreat.html

● THE FEARSOME PHALANX

The phalanx was a terrifying battle formation made up of a large block of fighting men with spears. The Spartans used short spears, but the Macedonians used huge spears called sarissas that were up to 21 ft. (6.5m) long. The front ranks pointed them forward. The rear held them up at angles to break the flights of arrows.

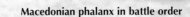

Macedonian phalanx in battle order

GREATER GREECE

HELLENISTIC—following the Greek way of life from 323 to 30 B.C.

After the death of Alexander in 323 B.C., the huge empire was fought over by his generals, who were hungry for power. In the end, it broke up into separate Greek-ruled kingdoms—Macedonia-Greece, Egypt, the Seleucid Empire (across the Middle East), and Pergamon in Asia Minor. These were stormy times, but the Greek way of life spread far and wide. This is known as the Hellenistic period of Greek history.

A Roman army uses elephants to scatter the Macedonian phalanx at the Battle of Cynoscephalae in Thessaly in 197 B.C.

The war elephants are armored, with metal tips on their tusks.

Elephants were widely used in warfare—they were the ancient equivalents of tanks.

The last Greek ruler of Egypt was a famous queen named Cleopatra, who died in 30 B.C.

GREEKS AND ASIANS

This stone carving in the Greek style belonged to a Buddhist monument from Gandhara, a kingdom in what is now Afghanistan and Pakistan. For centuries, Greek and Asian art and thought influenced each other in this region.

THE WELL-PLANNED CITY

Fine new cities were planned and built across the Hellenistic world, decorated with very realistic statues. Priene, on the coast of Asia Minor, was rebuilt in a regular grid pattern, with well-drained streets, magnificent temples, public buildings, a theater, and a sports stadium.

GREECE VERSUS ROME

In the 300s and 200s B.C., the Italian city of Rome became more and more powerful. It conquered the Greek colonies in Italy, and its armies soon marched into North Africa and western Asia. Macedonia was finally defeated in 168 B.C. after many battles, such as Cynoscephalae. After the Achaean War of 147–146 B.C., all of Greece came under Roman rule. The Greeks had lost their freedom—but their ways of life inspired the Romans as they in turn built cities and a great empire.

A BEACON IN THE NIGHT

This tall lighthouse was built in about 267 B.C. in Greek-ruled Egypt. It was located at the port of Alexandria, which was named after Alexander the Great. The city became a major center of learning and was famous for its large library.

GREEKS AND ROMANS

The first part of this memorial is written in the Greek language and letters. The second part is in Latin, the language of Rome. Many Romans could speak Greek, and the two Mediterranean peoples shared similar beliefs and customs.

GREEK LEGACY

Many different lands shaped the civilizations of ancient Greece, from Europe to western Asia and Egypt. Classical Greece provided the foundations for a new European culture, with its great achievements in philosophy, politics, mathematics, architecture, drama, and music. Even today, European languages are full of words that come from ancient Greek. Ideas from that distant period of history have spread around the modern world.

THE BYZANTINES

In 667 B.C., the Greeks founded a colony named Byzantium. In A.D. 330, the Romans built a fine new city on the site, calling it Constantinople (now named Istanbul). It became the eastern capital of the Roman Empire and thrived long after Rome had lost power, becoming the center of a Christian "Byzantine" Empire. Constantinople was captured by Muslim Turks in 1453. Greece won independence from Turkish rule in 1832.

The splendid Christian Church of Holy Wisdom was completed in A.D. 537. It later became a Muslim mosque, and it has been a museum since 1935.

Hagia Sophia, Istanbul

JUSTINIAN THE GREAT

Justinian I was emperor from A.D. 527 to 565. He set about winning back the lands of the western Roman Empire. In his own eastern empire, Roman law was still used, but people spoke Greek, and the empire's "Orthodox" forms of Christian worship developed separately from those of Rome.

The minarets (prayer towers) date from the building's period as a Turkish mosque.

THE GREAT REVIVAL

www.metmuseum.org/explore/byzantium/byz_1.html

Many ancient Greek ideas were respected by Christians in the Middle Ages. Precious records of their work were protected by scholars in the Muslim world. In the 1400s and 1500s, there was a great revival, or Renaissance, of interest in ancient Greece and Rome. Greek and Latin were taught in schools. Discoveries of sites such as Mycenae and Knossos fascinated new generations in the 1800s and 1900s.

Plato and Aristotle feature in this 1510–1511 painting by Raphael, an artist of the Italian Renaissance.

DEMOKRATÍA

The modern Greek parliament meets in Athens, where the idea of democracy was born more than 2,500 years ago. Modern governments may view democracy in many different ways, but most still claim that rule by the people is central to their ideals as a nation.

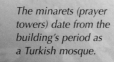

GLOSSARY

AGORA
The central market and business district in a Greek town; the forum.

ALL-IN COMBAT
Fighting, wrestling, and boxing at the same time.

ALTAR
A table or slab where offerings are made to a god or goddess.

ARCHAEOLOGIST
Someone who looks for ancient sites, making a methodical, scientific study of remains and ruins.

BRAZIER
A movable metal container for holding charcoal or burning wood.

BRONZE
A metal that is an alloy (mixture) of copper and tin and is used for making tools and weapons.

CHARIOT
A light cart, normally pulled by horses, used in warfare or sports.

CHORUS
A group of men who performed identical actions and speech during a theatrical performance.

CITY-STATE
A small, independent nation based on a single city and the surrounding region or island.

CONQUER
To defeat an enemy, often invading their lands.

DEMOCRACY
Rule by the people or by their representatives.

EMPIRE
A number of different lands controlled by a single ruler.

EPIC
A long and exciting story about heroic adventures.

FORTIFICATION
Walls, ditches, towers, or forts built for defense or attack.

GRID PATTERN
A town plan that has straight roads crossing each other at regular intervals.

HELMSMAN
The person who steers a boat or ship.

HIMATION
A large, loose cloak worn by both men and women in ancient Greece.

HOPLITE
An ancient Greek foot soldier armed with a spear, sword, and shield.

IMMORTAL
Someone who lives forever. A member of the Persian royal guard was called an Immortal because whenever one was killed in battle, another immediately took his place.

KILN
A very hot oven used to "fire" (bake and harden) pottery.

LOOM
A frame used for weaving cloth.

MINOAN

Belonging to the first great civilization on the island of Crete, from about 2700 to 1420 B.C.

MINT

1) To make metal coins; 2) the place where coins are made.

MOSAIC

A picture made from many small, colored tiles or fragments of pottery, stone, or glass.

MUSES

Nine goddesses or spirits believed to inspire activities such as music, dance, poetry, or drama. The words *music* and *museum* come from the word *mousieon*, a shrine to the muses.

MYCENAEAN

Belonging to the civilization that developed around the citadels of southern Greece from about 1600 to 1100 B.C.

OFFERING

A sacrifice or gift offered to a god or goddess, perhaps at a shrine or an altar.

ORCHESTRA

A performance space in front of the main stage used by the chorus in an ancient Greek theater.

ORTHODOX

Following a correct or traditional form of worship—as practiced, for example, by the Greek Orthodox Church.

POLITICS

The study or practice of government or ways of bringing about social change.

RITUAL

A ceremony or series of acts used in religion and worship.

SACRIFICE

A gift to a god or goddess. In ancient Greece it was usually an animal, such as a white bull, killed at an altar.

SARISSA

A very long spear used by a Macedonian phalanx in battle.

SCRIPT

A form of writing, such as an alphabet.

SHRINE

A holy place or temple.

SLAVE

Someone who has no freedom and who is bought, sold, and forced to work for no reward.

STATESMAN

A leading politician.

STERN

The back end of a boat or ship.

TRIDENT

A three-pronged spear. It is a symbol of the god Poseidon.

TRIREME

A warship with three banks of rowers.

WARE

A type or style of pottery.

YARN

Thread that has been spun from a loose fiber, such as wool. Women wove yarn into cloth for clothing, using large looms.

INDEX

INVESTIGATE

The world of ancient Greece may not be as far away as you think—just look in a museum, in a book, or on the stage or screen.

MUSEUMS AND EXHIBITIONS

In many countries around the world, especially in Europe, you will find museums displaying beautiful Greek pottery, statues, coins, or jewelry.

 Ancient Greece by Anne Pearson (Dorling Kindersley)

 The Metropolitan Museum of Art, 1000 Fifth Avenue, New York, NY 10028

ruins of the Temple of Poseidon, Sounion, Greece

 www.metmuseum.org

clay tablet showing a woman at a table from Locris, Greece

scene from a movie about Alexander the Great

ARCHAEOLOGY

If you are interested in archaeology, make a start by joining a local group for young people. If you someday go on vacation to Greece, Turkey, or southern Italy, you can even visit the ancient Greek sites for yourself.

 Greece by Stephen Biesty (Oxford University Press)

 Palace of Knossos, near Heraklion, Crete

www.digonsite.com and www.ancient-greece.org/archaeology.html

FICTION, STAGE, AND SCREEN

Myths, legends, and tales of ancient Greece have always inspired writers and filmmakers, and they can recreate the ancient magic just for you. Why not make Greek masks or put on a Greek play at your school?

Writings of the ancient Greek historian Herodotus can be read today.

 Black Ships Before Troy by Rosemary Sutcliffe (Frances Lincoln)

 Hercules DVD (Walt Disney Home Video)

 www.greektheatre.gr

RESEARCH

A visit to your local library is sure to offer information about ancient Greece.

 The Usborne Encyclopedia of Ancient Greece by Jane Chisholm (Usborne)

 Perseus Digital Library, Tufts University, Medford, MA 02155

 www.perseus.tufts.edu